MY ROYAL MILE ADVENTURE

Jan-Andrew Henderson

BLACK HART. EDINBURGH. BRISBANE.

Copyright © 2021 by Jan-Andrew Henderson.

All rights reserved. No part of this publication may be reproduced, distributed or transmitted in any form or by any means, including photocopying, recording, or other electronic or mechanical methods, without the prior written permission of the publisher, except in the case of brief quotations embodied in critical reviews and certain other non-commercial uses permitted by copyright law. For permission requests, write to the publisher, addressed "Attention: Permissions Coordinator," at the address below.

Jan-Andrew Henderson/Black Hart.

Redgum Close, Bellbowrie, Brisbane QLD 4070

www.janandrewhenderson.com

Cover by Jan-Andrew Henderson and Pamela Jeffs.

Images by Jan-Andrew Henderson. Line drawings by Emily Canter.

Publisher's Note: This is a work of fiction. Locales and public names are sometimes used for atmospheric purposes.

Book design © 2017, BookDesignTemplates.com

My Royal Mile Adventure. Jan-Andrew Henderson — First Edition.

ISBN 978-0-9928561-0-6 Paperback

ISBN 978-1-63625-848-5 eBook

Edinburgh Books by Jan-Andrew Henderson

The Royal Mile: A Comprehensive Guide

Edinburgh's Literary Heritage and How it Changed the World

Edinburgh New Town: A Comprehensive Guide

The Ghost That Haunted Itself

The Emperor's New Kilt

Edinburgh's Underground City

City of the Dead: The Fascinating Supernatural History of Edinburgh

In the heart of Edinburgh is a place you shouldn't miss

No other city in the world has somewhere quite like this

There's lots and lots of lots of treats

All squashed into one cobbled street

And if you don't explore it, then your visit's not complete

(It's only a mile long, so there's no excuse not to)

There's a palace at the bottom, a castle at the top

And dozens of attractions where you simply have to stop

To marvel at the history

And delve into its mystery

Or buy a tartan bonnet from the tartan bonnet shop

(You can even get one with ginger hair attached)

We started at the Castle - a truly awesome sight

It's a military garrison but they light it up at night

Every single day at one

The soldiers fire a big loud gun

Mum and dad fell over 'cause they both got such a fright.

(But I wasn't bothered. I was listening to my iPhone)

The Camera Obscura has weird effects galore

There are optical illusions on every single floor

Mirrors make you short or tall

Your head too big, your legs too small

Auntie Peg looked better than she ever did before

(She always was a funny shape)

The Mile has street performers who are there to entertain

We met the world's most piercy woman - she was called Elaine

Human statues never budge

Unless you give them a quick nudge

Or they need the toilet or it starts to pour with rain

(Then they move pretty quickly, I can tell you)

There are lots of narrow alleyways that never see the sun

They call them wynds or closes - Auntie Peg got stuck in one

Dad said. "Maybe you should diet"

Everyone went very quiet

It might well be the first time that I ever saw dad run

(No wonder. He moves like a girl)

The Heart of the Midlothian is a stone set in the ground

It's where a prison used to be before it got knocked down

All the locals stop and spit

On the very middle bit

If you're wearing sandals then it's best to go around

(But mum gave it a wipe because she's a clean freak)

Mary King's Close was very cool - we had a costumed guide

Who said that plague broke out there once and everybody died

Now it's buried underground

But you can still go look around

I washed my hands a dozen times when I got back outside

(Well, there's no point in taking chances, is there?)

St Giles' Cathedral has a crowned spire on its tower

A monument to show the church's dignity and power

Auntie Peg knelt down to pray

But then both of her knees gave way

She rolled under the pulpit and was stuck there for an hour

(We thought she was planking, at first)

At night we took a ghost tour called *City of the Dead*

Into Greyfriars Graveyard, which quite messed up my head

It had a poltergeist, they claimed

And visitors get bit and maimed

I ended up with nightmares and slept in my parents' bed

(Serves them right for taking me in the first place)

The Mile is lined with tourist shops all selling tartan gear

Granddad bought some whisky and then he disappeared

We found him on the Royal Mile

Wearing nothing but a smile

Singing *Flower of Scotland* while a crowd all clapped and cheered

(The street performers offered to give him a daily slot)

We found a small museum that was full of ancient toys!

Pink ones for the little girls

Blue ones for the boys

Clockwork trains and candy canes, creepy dolls and model planes

Dad said they're the kind of thing that every kid enjoys

(Really? I didn't see an X-Box in there)

Our Dynamic Earth displayed how all of life began

Starting with the dinosaurs, right up to modern man

I asked granddad if he was there

And he gave me quite a stare

Then he winked at us and said, "You better ask your gran."

(She did more than give him a stare. Ouch.)

We visited the palace, so Granddad wore a suit

We asked to see the queen but the guard said, "Naw, she's oot."

I said I was her missing heir

She wouldn't mind me staying there

I don't think he believed it but he gave me a salute

(Mum was surprised I didn't get arrested)

Next door is the parliament that rules the Scottish nation

Gran got lost and ended up leading a demonstration

She threw her bag at the police

And got charged with breach of the peace

Then claimed it was the best moment of her entire vacation

(Granddad didn't talk to her for a week)

At the bottom of the Royal Mile, we climbed up Arthur's Seat

It's an extinct volcano, now *that* is pretty neat

We fed bread to the ducks and swans

Granddad fell into a pond

And mum and dad both ended up with blisters on their feet

(Auntie Peg didn't even attempt it)

So that was our adventure and, boy, we had a ball!

We bought this little book as a reminder of it all

And brought it back so we could show

The places that you ought to go

Will you have the same adventure? Well, you never know…

(Say hello to Elaine if you do)

The Attractions

The Royal Mile

The main street of Edinburgh's historic Old Town, built on a high glaciated ridge overlooking the rest of the city.

Edinburgh Castle

King David I (1084-1153) was instrumental in erecting the impressive fortifications you see today. But it continued to be added to right up until the 20th century. It is now Scotland's most popular visitor attraction

Camera Obscura

This attraction features one of only two working Victorian camera obscuras in Scotland (the other is Kirriemuir). It has been in operation for over 150 years. It is on top of several floors of optical illusions and next to The Tartan Weaving Centre.

The Edinburgh Festival and Fringe

Every August, the Royal Mile is filled with street performers as part of the world's largest arts festival. Established in 1947 there is now a book and film festival and thousands of shows in the 'Festival Fringe' across hundreds of venues - including street performances.

Side Streets

The Royal Mile has many narrow alleyways called wynds and closes, caused by terrible overcrowding in the past. They often open onto living spaces called courts and are well worth exploring.

Heart of Midlothian

This stone heart marks the site of the entrance to the Old Tolbooth. Built in 1561 as a customs house for merchants, it became the Town Hall, then a prison and place of execution. It is customary for people to spit on the stone as a sign of disrespect.

Mary King's Close

An entire street underneath the City Chambers and part of Edinburgh's legendary Underground City. It became famous as a haunted area after plague ravaged it in 1645. However, it was still occupied until the early 20th century.

St Giles' Cathedral

Named after a sixth-century French monk, there has been a church here since antiquity. In the middle are four massive central pillars that date from 1120. The square outside was a place of public execution and the guillotine was kept in the cathedral.

City of the Dead Tours/Greyfriars Kirkyard

Greyfriars is a 16th-century walled graveyard where many famous people are buried. It is haunted by the legendary Mackenzie Poltergeist, which can be investigated on a *City of the Dead* tour.

The Writers' Museum

Situated in Lady Stairs Close, The Writers' Museum celebrates the lives and works of three of Scotland's most famous writers – Robert Burns, Sir Walter Scott and Robert Louis Stevenson. All of them lived in Edinburgh and hung out on the Royal Mile.

The Museum of Childhood

A free museum of children's toys, dating from Victorian, Edwardian and Georgian times to the present day. If you like creepy dolls with staring eyes that follow you around the room, you'll have a blast.

Our Dynamic Earth

This attraction is the story of planet earth, from the big bang to the present day. Opened in 1999, it is an unusual structure, with a membrane stretched on steel poles forming a roof over the remains of a former brewery.

Holyrood Palace

Still the official royal residence in Scotland, the most famous inhabitant was Mary Queen of Scots in the 16th century. Bonnie Prince Charlie also stayed there during his 18th century attempt to regain the throne of Britain.

The Scottish Parliament

Built between 1999 and 2004, the most famous part is the modernist debating chamber with an impressive ceiling made from tensile steel wires and oak beams.

Arthur's Seat

Part of 650-acre Holyrood Park, Arthur's Seat is the main peak of the group of hills that form most of Holyrood Park. It is the highest point in Edinburgh, with magnificent views of the city.

Jan-Andrew Henderson is the author of 33 children's, teen, YA, adult and non-fiction books. Published in the UK, USA, Australia, Canada and Europe, he has been shortlisted for thirteen literary awards and is the winner of the Doncaster Book Prize and the Royal Mail Award.

An ex guide, he owns City of the Dead Tours in Edinburgh.

www.janandrewhenderson.com

www.cityofthedeadtours.com